LIFESAVING

D1511044

BOY SCOUTS OF AMERICA
IRVING, TEXAS

**1994 Printing of the
1993 Edition**

Note to the Counselor

There are several merit badges in Boy Scouting that prepare the Scout for immediate service. First Aid is one; Lifesaving is another. The requirements for these merit badges are meant to reflect an understanding on the part of the boy consistent with the safe performance of this service. The well-being not only of the accident victim but also of the rescuer depends on this understanding. It is your responsibility as counselor to approve only those who meet the merit badge requirements. Furthermore, since a misconception is often worse than no training at all, it is your responsibility to continue to guide those whose performance is initially inadequate. At the very least, the boy must understand why his performance is not yet acceptable. A lack of approval will not prevent the Boy Scout from acting in time of need to the best of his ability. You must ensure that the techniques he will use are proper for the situation.

The techniques that are deemed proper are those outlined in this pamphlet. In line with general policy, requirements must not be added or deleted at your discretion. Several organizations offer excellent lifesaving courses. These should be encouraged as supplements to the Scout's training. They are not, however, to serve as substitutes for the Lifesaving merit badge.

The minimum time required for training is that which leaves the Scout prepared. No definite time limits are established. It is expected that adequate in-water training will be given the boy before the requirements are attempted. Further guidance is available in section IV, "Aquatics," in *Camp Program and Property Management,* available through your local council service center.

Copyright 1993
Boy Scouts of America
Irving, Texas
ISBN 0-8395-3297-0
No. 33297   Printed in U.S.A.   18M1094

Requirements

1. Before doing requirements 2–15

   a. Earn the Swimming merit badge.

   b. Swim 400 yards.

2. Explain

   a. Safe Swim Defense and Safety Afloat

   b. The order of methods in water rescue

3. Show reaching rescues using such things as arms, legs, branches, sticks, towels, shirts, paddles, and poles.

4. Show rescues using items that can be thrown, such as lines, ring buoys, rescue bags, and free-floating supports.

5. Show or explain the use of rowboats, canoes, and other small craft in making rescues.

6. With a helper and a practice victim, show a line rescue both as tender and as rescuer. Perform the rescue with the practice victim approximately thirty feet from the tender. Use a 100-foot length of $\frac{3}{16}$-inch line.

7. Show that you can remove street clothes* on shore (except underwear or swim trunks) in 20 seconds or less. Explain the importance of disrobing before a swimming rescue.

8. Explain the importance of avoiding contact with a victim; explain "lead" and "wait" tactics; and explain why equipment should be used in a swimming rescue.

9. Swim 30 feet and make the correct approach to a tired swimmer. Move him 30 feet to safety using the following:

   a. Underarm swim-along

   b. Two-person assist

---

*"Street clothes" means low shoes, socks, underwear (or trunks), pants, belt, and long-sleeve shirt. A jacket, sweater, or sweatshirt also may be worn.

10. Make rescues on a practice victim 30 feet from shore, using the correct entry and a strong approach stoke, and bringing the victim back to pier or poolside, using

    a. A rescue tube or torpedo buoy

    b. A shirt, towel, or other equipment

    c. A front approach and wrist tow

    d. A rear approach and single armpit tow

    e. A rear approach and single armpit tow, changing to the cross-chest carry

    Discuss the different methods for removing a victim from the water. Choose the appropriate method for your situation. Remove the practice victim from the water and place in position for resuscitation.

11. Show in deep water your defense against grasps by blocking and escaping. Free yourself from a wrist hold, rear head-hold, and a front head-hold.

12. Make four surface dives in 8 to 10 feet of water. Retrieve an object on each of the first three dives. Bring up a 10-pound weight on the fourth dive.

13. Show search techniques as part of a lost-swimmer drill. Discuss search techniques using mask, fins, and snorkel (not scuba).

14. Do the following:

    a. Identify the conditions that must exist before performing CPR on a person, and explain how such conditions are recognized.

    b. Demonstrate proper technique for performing CPR on an adult mannequin for at least 3 minutes.

15. Demonstrate proper management of a spinal injury by

    a. Explaining the signs and symptoms of a spinal injury

    b. Supporting a faceup victim in calm, shallow water

    c. Turning a person from a facedown to a faceup position while maintaining support

Contents

Acknowledgments

The Boy Scouts of America expresses its appreciation to David Bell, Albert E. Cahill, William S. Hurst, E. D. Schermerhorn, and K. Gregory Tucker for their efforts in compiling the material and writing the contents of this pamphlet.

To Help Other People at All Times

No Boy Scout will ignore a plea for help. However, the desire to help is of little use unless you can give the proper aid. The primary purpose of the Lifesaving merit badge is to prepare you to give assistance to those involved in water accidents. Since drowning is the second major cause of accidental deaths for the Scouting age group in the United States, this training can indeed prepare you to save a life.

If you have completed the First Aid and Swimming merit badges, then you have already gained some of the skills necessary to aid a person in distress in the water. More important, you should have begun to realize that the ability to think under stress, to keep your cool, is your greatest asset. Action without thought is not only wasted, but in some cases, dangerous. A life-or-death situation is no time for confusion or false dramatics. Rescues should be performed with little fanfare in the easiest and safest manner possible. Only in this way can you ensure the safety of the victim and yourself.

You have probably seen and admired the work of lifeguards at the local swimming pool. The Lifesaving merit badge prepares you to protect yourself and others in the water. A lifesaver is concerned with personal safety, how to prevent accidents, and how to protect themselves in an emergency. However, a lifeguard is taught that their first concern is the safety of others. Additional training, beyond this merit badge, is required to qualify you as a lifeguard. The lifesaving merit badge prepares you to be a lifesaver, not a lifeguard.

Preparation

If you read this pamphlet carefully, you will learn what "easiest and safest" entails. However, many of the skills cannot be learned without actual physical demonstration and practice. Your counselor, therefore, will instruct you in the various skills before expecting you to meet the requirements. You can begin now to prepare for this instruction.

First, read the pamphlet so that you will know what is to be covered and why. This will allow you to gain the most from the expertise of your instructor. Second, begin to swim regularly until you can complete the required distance swim with ease. Physical stamina is required for some rescue techniques.

Once you begin to receive instruction, practice will be essential. Indeed, to remain a proficient lifesaver, some skills must be reviewed throughout your life. Before practicing with a buddy, make sure you understand the correct technique. Ask your counselor to repeat any demonstrations that were not clear. Proceed slowly and deliberately until the movement becomes natural. Only then should you work for speed. Be realistic. A buddy who knows what you are about to do can perform movements an actual accident victim could never execute. However, realism can be carried too far. Do not use the word "help" as a practice signal. Lifeguards have their ears tuned to this word and will automatically give you their attention when it might be needed elsewhere. Also, arrange a signal with your buddy that means "Let go, I need to catch my breath."

With practice, you can easily master the skills required for this merit badge. Keep in mind however that you are also expected to understand when these skills are to be applied. Be alert to all that is said. Your instructor will not cover material that is not important. Lifesaving is a serious undertaking and must be treated accordingly.

Topics to Be Covered

Aquatic activities are the pastime of millions and the livelihood of many others. Although the number of people entering the water increases every year, the number of water-related fatalities has remained fairly constant, at about seven thousand annually for many years. This can only mean that people are better prepared now than they were in the past. Training such as that received for the Lifesaving merit badge is part of the reason. Three different approaches can be taken to further reduce the number of fatalities: (1) accident prevention, (2) self-preservation, and (3) training to assist others. We will consider each of these in turn.

Accident Prevention

Lifesaving begins with the prevention of water-related accidents. The safety of an aquatics area should be judged by how few emergencies arise rather than by the number of assists successfully performed. The prepared lifesaver reacts to situations of potential danger long before they become a problem.

Every Scout a Swimmer

The best way to prevent accidents is to study their causes. Most people who drown are unskilled swimmers. If everyone could swim well, the number of drownings would decrease. If there are members of your family or troop who can not swim, it is your duty to encourage them to learn.

Remind them that thousands who drown each year had no intention of entering the water. Once a person becomes adjusted to the water, many types of recreational activities will present themselves. Learning to swim involves fun as well as safety. Steps for teaching the nonswimmer can be found in your *Boy Scout Handbook*.

Safe Swim Defense

If you were to study actual cases of drowning during recreational swims, you would notice several common factors. These would include a lack of adequate supervision, as in the case of a small child wandering into deep water, physical problems such as a heart attack, and often the use of an unsafe area as shown by the poor swimmer stepping unexpectedly into a deep hole or the diver hitting his head on a submerged object. Having found these contributory causes of drowning, you could then establish rules or procedures for avoiding them. Add to your list a few precautionary instructions on what to do if an accident does happen, and you will have a set of guidelines with which to conduct a safe swim period while allowing everyone the maximum enjoyment of the water. Such a set of guidelines, called the Safe Swim Defense, has been developed for use during troop swims. With only a few adjustments, it also can be used whenever you swim with family or friends.

The Safe Swim Defense has eight parts:

1. **Qualified Supervision.** All swimming activity must be supervised by a mature and conscientious adult over 21 years of age who understands and knowingly accepts responsibility for the well-being and safety of the children in his or her care, who is experienced in the water and confident of his or her ability to respond in the event of an emergency, and who is trained in and committed to compliance with the eight points of BSA Safe Swim Defense. (It is strongly recommended that all units have at least one adult or older youth member currently certified as a BSA Lifeguard to assist in the planning and conduct of all swimming activity.)

2. **Physical Fitness.** Require evidence of fitness for swimming activity with a complete health history from physician, parent, or legal guardian. The adult supervisor should adjust all supervision, discipline, and protection to anticipate any potential risks associated with individual health conditions. In the event of any significant health conditions, proof of an examination by a physician should be required by the unit leader.

3. **Safe Area.** Have lifeguards and swimmers systematically examine the bottom of the swimming area to determine varying depths, deep holes, rocks, and stumps. Mark off the area for three groups: not more than 3½ feet deep for nonswimmers; from shallow water to just over the head for beginners; deep water not over 12 feet for swimmers. For boundary markers use poles stuck in the bottom, or plastic bottles, balloons, or sticks attached to rock anchors with twine. Enclose nonswimmer and beginner areas with buoy lines (twine and floats) between markers. Mark the outer bounds of the swimmer area with floats. Diving from the edge of pools, piers, or floating platforms requires a minimum water depth of 7 feet.

4. **Lifeguards on Duty.** Designate two capable swimmers as lifeguards. Station them ashore, equipped with a lifeline (a 100-foot length of ³⁄₁₆-inch nylon cord). In an emergency, one carries out the line and the other feeds it out from shore, then pulls in his partner and the boy being assisted. In addition, if a boat is available, man it with two persons, preferably capable swimmers, one rowing and the other equipped with a 10-foot pole or extra oar. Provide one guard for every ten boys.

5. **Lookout.** Station a lookout on the shore where he can see and hear everything in all areas. He can be the adult in charge of the swim and can give the buddy signals.

6. **Ability Groups.** Divide the boys into three ability groups: nonswimmers, beginners, and swimmers. Keep each group in its own area. Nonswimmers have not passed any swimming test. Beginners must have passed this test: jump feetfirst into water over their head in depth, level off, swim 25 feet on the surface, turn sharply, resume swimming as before, and return to the starting place. Swimmers must have passed this test: jump feetfirst into water over their head in depth, level off, and begin swimming. Swim 75 yards in a strong manner, using one or more of the following strokes: sidestroke, breaststroke, trudgen, or crawl; then swim 25 yards using an easy, resting backstroke. The 100 yards must be swum continuously and include at least one sharp turn. After completing the swim, rest by floating as motionlessly as possible. *These classification tests should be renewed annually, preferably at the beginning of each season.*

Safe Swim Defense
1. Qualified supervision
2. Physical fitness
3. Safe area
4. Lifeguards on duty
5. Lookout
6. Ability groups
7. Buddy system
8. Discipline

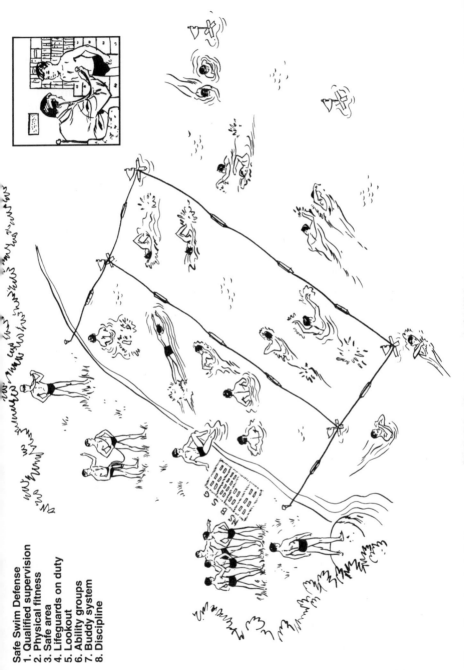

7. **Buddy System.** Pair every boy with another in his own ability group. Buddies check in and out of the swimming area together. Check all boys in the water about every ten minutes. The adult in charge signals for a buddy check with a single blast of a whistle or ring of a bell and a call of "Buddies!" He counts slowly to ten while buddies join and raise hands and remain still and silent. Guards check all areas, count the pairs, and compare the total with the number known to be in the water. Signal two blasts or bells to resume swimming. Signal three blasts or bells for checkout.

8. **Discipline.** Be sure all Scouts and Explorers understand and agree that swimming is allowed only with proper supervision and use of the complete Safe Swim Defense. Advise their parents of this policy. When the Scouts know the reason for rules and procedures, they are more likely to follow them. Be strict and fair, showing no favoritism.

The Safe Swim Defense should be familiar to you. It is in your *Boy Scout Handbook* and is included in the requirements for the Swimming merit badge. You might wonder if all the repetition is really necessary; indeed, you might think that the whole concept is more of a bother than it is worth. You might sometimes object to the responsibilities and minor restrictions imposed by the buddy system. A beginner might wonder why he is not allowed to jump into deep water from the diving board since he can make it to the side with his excellent dog paddle. Besides that, no one ever gets into trouble at a supervised swim anyway. Or do they? The answer can be found in the accident reports.

Very seldom does anyone get into trouble, and those people are quickly assisted, if the plan is followed. However, this excellent record can lead to a false sense of security. With no accidents to spoil the fun, the points of the Safe Swim Defense are sometimes relaxed, or even ignored. Unfortunately, this all too often proves the need for strict adherence. Quite simply, the necessity for every point of the plan has to be, and continues to be, proven in the worst possible way—by the needless loss of life.

Safety Afloat

It was mentioned earlier that many drowning victims did not intend to enter the water. Automobile accidents, floods, and, sometimes, just falling into the water account for many of these drownings. Boating accidents cause many others. Just as the ability to swim will save people thrown into the water, the ability to handle a boat properly will prevent an unexpected swim. The other aquatic merit badge pamphlets will give you information on handling the various craft and the safety precautions necessary for each. A set of safety guidelines similar to Safe Swim Defense, but only for boating activities, is known as Safety Afloat.

1. **Qualified Supervision.** All activity afloat must be supervised by a mature and conscientious adult over 21 years of age who understands and knowingly accepts responsibility for the well-being and safety of the children in his or her care, who is experienced and qualified in the particular watercraft skills and equipment involved in the activity, and who is committed to compliance with the nine points of BSA Safety Afloat. One such supervisor is required for each ten people, with a minimum of two adults for any one group. All supervisors must complete BSA Safety Afloat and Safe Swim Defense training, and at least one must be certified in CPR. (It is strongly recommended that all units have at least one adult or older youth member currently certified as a BSA Lifeguard to assist in the planning and conduct of all activity afloat.)

   For Cub Scouts: The ratio of adult supervisors to Cub Scouts is one to five.

2. **Physical Fitness.** All participants must present evidence of fitness assured by a complete health history from a physician, parent, or legal guardian. Adjust all supervision, discipline, and protection to anticipate any potential risks associated with individual health conditions. In the event of any significant health conditions, a medical evaluation by a physician should be required by the adult leader.

3. **Swimming Ability.** A person who has not been classified as a "swimmer" may ride as a passenger in a rowboat or motorboat with an adult swimmer, or in a canoe, raft, or sailboat with an adult certified as a lifeguard or a lifesaver by a recognized agency. In all other circumstances, the person must be a "swimmer" to participate in an activity afloat. Swimmers must pass this test: Jump feetfirst into water over the head in depth, level off, and begin swimming. Swim 75 yards in a *strong* manner, using one or more of the following strokes: sidestroke, breaststroke, trudgen, or crawl; then swim 25 yards using an easy, resting backstroke. The 100 yards must be swum continuously and include at least one sharp turn. After completing the swim, rest by floating. *This qualification test should be renewed annually.*

4. **Personal Flotation Equipment.** Properly fitted U.S. Coast Guard–approved personal flotation devices (PFDs) must be worn by all persons engaged in activity on the open water (rowing, canoeing, sailing, boardsailing, motorboating, waterskiing, rafting, tubing, kayaking, and surfboarding). Type II and III PFDs are recommended.

5. **Buddy System.** All activity afloat necessitates using the buddy system. Not only does every individual have a buddy, but every craft should have a buddy boat when on the water.

6. **Skill Proficiency.** All persons participating in activity afloat must be trained and experienced in watercraft handling skills, safety, and emergency procedures.

   a. For unit activity on white water, all participants must complete special training by a BSA Aquatics Instructor or qualified whitewater specialist.

   b. Powerboat operators must be able to meet requirements for the Motorboating merit badge or equivalent.

c. A minimum of 3 hours training and supervised practice is required for all other unpowered watercraft.

For Cub Scouts: Canoeing and rafting for Cub Scouts (including Webelos Scouts) is to be limited to council/district events on flatwater ponds or controlled lake areas free of powerboats and sailboats. Prior to recreational canoeing, Cub Scouts are to be instructed in basic handling skills and safety practices.

7. Planning:

Float Plan. Obtain current maps and information about the waterway to be traveled. Know exactly where the unit will "put in" and "pull out" and which course will be followed. Travel time should be estimated generously. Review the plan with others who have traveled the course recently.

Local Rules. Determine which state and local regulations are applicable, and follow them. Get written permission to use or cross private property.

Notification. File the float plan with the parents of the participants and a member of the unit committee. File the float plan with the local council service center if you'll be traveling on running water. Check in with all those notified when you return.

Weather. Check the weather forecast just before setting out and keep an alert weather eye. Bring all craft ashore when rough weather threatens.

Contingencies. Planning must identify possible emergencies or other circumstances that could force a change of plans. Appropriate alternative plans must be developed for each.

For Cub Scouts: Cub Scout canoeing and rafting does not include "trips" or "expeditions" and is not to be conducted on running water (i.e., rivers or streams); therefore, some procedures are inapplicable. Suitable weather requires clear skies, warm air and water, and no appreciable wind.

8. Equipment.
All equipment must be suited to the craft, the water conditions, and the individual; must be in good repair; and must satisfy all state and federal requirements. Spare equipment or repair materials must be carried. Appropriate rescue equipment must be available for immediate use.

9. Discipline. All participants should know, understand, and respect the rules and procedures for a safe activity afloat. Rules for safety do not interfere with fun when fairly applied.

Note: For cruising vessels (excluding rowboats, canoes, kayaks, and rafts, but including sailboats and powerboats greater than 20 feet long) used in adult-supervised unit activities by a chartered Explorer post/ship specializing in watercraft operations, or used in adult-supervised program activity in connection with any high-adventure program or other activity under the direct sponsorship and control of the National Council, the standards and procedures in the *Sea Exploring Manual* may be substituted for the Safety Afloat standards.

Personal Survival

In lifesaving, as well as in medicine, prevention is better than the cure. However, just as a doctor must know how to treat an illness if it is contracted, the lifesaver must know how to react during an emergency. The first emergencies we will consider are those in which you might play a double role—that of victim as well as rescuer.

The importance of adequate swimming skill has been mentioned. The accomplished swimmer should master a variety of strokes. The crawl is excellent for covering distance rapidly, but too much speed in swimming, as on the highway, wastes energy. This shortens the distance a person can travel in time of need. Many drownings can be blamed on simple exhaustion. The breaststroke, sidestroke, and elementary backstroke, on the other hand, are restful strokes. If properly done, the swimmer does not have to be a conditioned athlete to cover long distances in an emergency. In addition, these strokes can still be used if an arm or leg is disabled.

The better you swim, the more relaxed and confident you will be in the water. This will allow you to handle situations that might cause panic in others. One such situation is a cramp.

Cramps

A cramp is when a muscle, usually in the leg or foot, unexpectedly tightens. A cramp can be painful and temporarily prevent use of the limb. There is little danger, however, unless you panic. A change of body position or swimming stroke often will provide complete relief when tingles are first felt. Otherwise, float facedown and stretch the cramped muscle. Squeezing the area will help reduce the pain. The cramp will stop soon.

River Currents

A more dangerous situation arises when a swimmer is caught in a current. Remain calm and do not fight against the water. In a river clear of obstructions swim across the current. This will eventually move you to the bank, perhaps quite a bit downstream from your original destination, but none the worse for wear.

The same general idea works in white water. Here, however, there is definite danger of striking a rock or other obstruction. Float feetfirst downstream. Try to keep all of your body at the surface. You can ride the rapids in this manner, or "fin" with your hands to move yourself into quiet water. Do not try to stand or to climb onto an obstruction from the upstream side. You could be crushed against a rock

In rapids, float feetfirst downstream.

or trapped beneath a log. The flow of water around an exposed rock will generally keep you clear if you assume the feetfirst position. You might even find yourself drawn into a quiet area or eddy behind a rock. This will allow you to climb out of the water from the downstream side and wait for help.

An extreme danger develops just below a waterfall or low water dam, where the water is continuously rolling. An object or person cast into such a *roller* or *hydraulic* will be repeatedly tumbled. The churning water is full of bubbles which makes it difficult to catch a breath and very hard to swim. If you remain calm there are two ways to escape from such a trap. One is to swim or push yourself along the length of the roller to shore or out the end of the roller to smooth water. The other is to dive to the bottom and swim downstream underwater where there is a downstream flow of water from the bottom of the roller.

Hydraulic—upstream surface current, downstream flow at bottom

Ocean Currents

Rips and *runouts* are strong currents caused by the seaward flow of water cast upon a beach by the surf. They can carry the unwary swimmer many yards offshore. If caught in an ocean current, use the same strategy employed in a river. Swim across the current, perpendicular to the beach. The currents generally are not very wide. When clear, swim for the shore. This is one of the situations where restful swimming strokes are needed.

Set, or *drift,* currents will not carry you out to sea but can wash you down the beach into areas of potential danger. Check occasionally to see if you are drifting.

An *undertow* causes no real danger for a good swimmer. It is a backwash of water after a breaking wave that can make it difficult to keep your footing. The rushing water will tend to wash the sand from beneath your feet and may create a shelf with a slight drop. You can slowly walk against the current or swim on the surface if the water is deep enough. The outward current will stop for a while with the next wave. Obviously, an undertow can cause problems for a small child or nonswimmer.

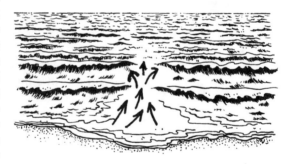

Rip—strong current running out from shore

Survival Floating

What if you were washed out to sea by a runout farther than you felt you could swim? Or perhaps because of a boating accident you found yourself in the water at night with no idea of the direction to safety? In such cases, you must be able to stay afloat until help arrives. Treading water will not work for long. In fact, it takes more energy than a restful swimming stroke. Floating on your back is fine, but can be difficult in waves. An alternative is survival floating. This is a skill you learned for the Swimming merit badge. Remember? Let's have a quick review.

First, take a breath to fill your lungs. Then float in a relaxed, facedown position, the "jellyfish" float. For most people, the back of the neck will break the surface. After holding your breath for a comfortable time, slowly spread your legs and lift your arms in the water. Then exhale beneath the surface as you bring your legs together and push gently downward with your arms. This will allow you to raise your head just above the surface. Since you exhaled on the way up, you are now ready to take another breath. Next, lower your head, relax, and repeat the cycle.

Several different arm and leg movements are possible. A backward thrust will allow slow progress toward shore. The main concern is not precision, but rather, slow, relaxed motion to conserve energy. It might help to pretend you are in shark-infested waters and must not make any quick movements so you won't become an unwilling dinner guest.

When you first learn to survival float, you might have trouble because you'll want to keep your head above the water more than beneath the surface. You might want to tread water while taking a long breath. No one can keep this up for long; the head is too heavy. If you doubt this, try holding a 10- or 15-pound weight out of the water. You might be surprised at the result, but that is about what your head weighs.

Survival floating

Survival floating is a warm-water skill; see the discussion on hypothermia for what to do if you find yourself in cold water (below 70° F).

Clothes Inflation

Inflation of clothing is an important self-rescue and survival skill, as you learned when working on the Swimming merit badge. If you ever fall overboard from a boat far from shore, your clothing can be used for supporting you at the surface until assistance arrives.

If you're wearing a cotton shirt or other closely woven material (not wool), grip it tightly at the neck. The air imprisoned in the back and shoulder areas will keep you afloat for a time. More air can be blown in through the front opening between the second and third buttons. Just bend your head down, pull the shirt opening to your mouth and blow air into the shirt. It will move to the back and form the supporting bubble. It helps to have your collar button fastened and your shirttail tucked in.

Pants of closely woven material can be turned into an effective PFD. Keep your shirt on for warmth while inflating your pants for support. Begin by removing your shoes while in the survival floating position, then carefully remove your pants. Do not turn them inside out. Next, inflate a pocket with a puff of air, or insert your hand, spread your fingers and lift the pocket clear of the water. The pocket will support the pants should you lose contact. Return to your floating position and tie the pant legs together as near the ends as you can. Pull the knot tight and then close the fly. The pants are now ready for inflation.

There are several ways to force air into the pants. Splashing air into the pants is the first choice and is probably the quickest and easiest means of inflation, but it might take some practice before you can do it well. Learn the skill by standing in chest-deep water. Hold the waistband open just below the surface, cup your hand in the air, and strike the water just in front of the pants. Follow through so that the air caught by your hand enters the opening of the pants. You should move the air just below the surface and then sideways so that it bubbles upward into the pants. The method will not work if you fail to lift your hand clear of the water or if you strike directly downward.

A second method is to place the pants behind your shoulder, hold the waistband open, and flip the pants overhead. This should fill them about half full. Repeat the flip only if unsuccessful; you will lose air already gained if you try to insert more air by this technique. Finish inflating the pants by splashing air into the pants using the method described above.

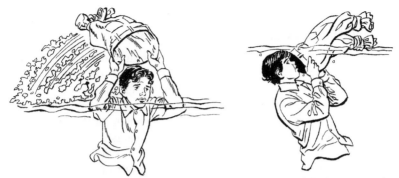

If you have difficulty in an emergency, you can fill the pants by blowing air into them from beneath. However, do not risk tiring yourself by hyperventilating.

When the pants are inflated, grasp the waist with the fly down and facing you. Place your head through the opening between the pant legs. Rest your head on the knot, lie back, and relax. If you have a belt, pull it tight with the loops bunched at the center. This will hold the waist closed and should provide sufficient length for you to run the belt around one of your legs and refasten. Your hands are now free for signaling or slowly swimming a backstroke toward shore.

Air will escape from your pants if you allow the material to dry. Splash water over them occasionally. When needed, additional air can be added simply by loosening the waist and splashing in air; the pants need not be removed. If the sun is bright, cover your head with your shirt to prevent sunburn. If more than one person is to be supported by the pants, have them hold on with their hands and lean backward in a floating position. Do not force the pants any deeper than necessary. Shorts can also be used for support by inflating the pockets, holding the shorts against your chest, and leaning backward.

Hypothermia

We have reviewed two techniques for staying afloat for extended periods of time. However, survival can depend on other factors, notably on the temperature of the water. Water conducts heat about twenty-five times better than air. Temperatures that are only uncomfortable in air will, in water, cause rapid lowering of the body's core temperature. Progressive loss of body heat will cause shivering, loss of movement, grogginess, unconsciousness, and death. In water, the loss of movement or consciousness may result in drowning before fatal body temperatures are reached.

The onset of hypothermia, or critical loss of body heat, depends on several factors. It is therefore difficult to say exactly how long a person can survive in water of a given temperature. A slender, lightly clothed person who has been exercising heavily, as in a canoe race, might die within minutes of a capsize in water below 5° C (40° F). On the other hand, a heavily clothed person with a flotation device might survive more than an hour in water of the same temperature. Thus, physical condition, clothing, and activity all affect a person's cooling rate.

If you are close enough to shore, get out of the cold water immediately. If, however, the distance to shore will require undue physical effort, wait for help. Although exercise will generate heat, the increased water circulation will conduct the heat away faster than it is replaced. In very cold water, even a 100-yard swim is impractical for a good swimmer.

HELP—heat escaping lessening posture

In a boating mishap, climb as far out of the water as possible. If you are alone and forced to wait for help in the water, assume a *heat escape lessening posture* (HELP), as pictured. If you are with several people, you should *huddle* together with each of your sides in contact. A PFD is essential for maximum survival time. If without one, inflate your shirt or jacket. Your head must stay clear of the water since it is a major area of heat loss.

Hypothermia refers to a low body temperature, specifically a low core temperature (temperature of the vital organs). Hypothermia occurs when cold or cool temperatures cause the body to lose heat faster than it can be produced and the body core temperature falls below normal.

Huddle position

Young swimmers under age 12 are especially vulnerable to cold water. Be alert to individuals showing the first signs of hypothermia, such as bluish lips or shivering. These swimmers should be moved to a warm area. Keep them in an area where there is little air movement, such as an office, first aid room, or tent. Cover them with a blanket until the hypothermia symptoms disappear. You may give warm liquids. Do not give alcoholic beverages or any containing caffeine.

Hypothermia can occur in less dramatic instances than capsizing in very cold water. You might have experienced the beginning stages of hypothermia on a cool day after swimming. During the first stage of hypothermia, the victim is still conscious and alert but is experiencing vigorous uncontrollable shivering. The ability to perform simple tasks is impaired.

As the body's core temperature drops, the victim's mental faculties and speech are impaired. The voice is weaker. There is loss of coordination. The victim performs simple tasks with much difficulty. Shivering lessens.

With further body core heat loss, the victim's mental faculties are severely impaired. The victim might be unconscious. Shivering is replaced by muscle rigidity (stiffness). The victim's skin might become bluish. Respiration and pulse become slower. The victim is totally unable to perform simple tasks.

When you observe signs of severe hypothermia, the victim should be handled as carefully as possible. Do not allow the victim to move around after being removed from the water. Do not rub or massage the victim's extremities. Call for help immediately. Maintain an open airway, if necessary. Prevent further heat loss. Allow the body temperature to return to normal gradually. Provide warm, dry clothing. Wrap the victim in blankets, dry towels, several layers of clothing, or all of these items. Avoid touching the victim with hot objects. If available, hot-water bottles, heating pads, or chemical heat packs can be used, but they should be wrapped in a towel or blanket to prevent them from burning the victim. They should be used to rewarm only the trunk, groin, neck, and head, since these areas of the body have the highest rates of heat loss. These areas, however, also transfer warmth to the body core faster than the extremities. Do not apply warming items, such as heating pads, to the extremities. Give warm liquids, such as broth, if the victim is conscious and able to swallow. Do not give liquids to an unconscious victim. Do not allow the victim to smoke. Do not give the victim any alcoholic beverages or any beverages containing caffeine. See that the victim receives immediate medical care.

When the body temperature begins to drop, the body reacts to correct the heat loss. The body reduces the flow of blood to the extremities in an attempt to prevent further heat loss. Shivering is an example of the body's efforts to increase heat production. Pay attention to the warning signs your body is giving you to stay out of danger.

Rescue Techniques

If you encounter a swimmer in need, take a few seconds to assess the situation and remember your training. Remain calm. Someone else might have already started a rescue. If so, stand out of the way ready to help. Pinpoint the victim's position from shore. Make sure medical aid has been summoned if needed. Keep curious bystanders from interfering with the rescue effort. If no one else is attempting a rescue, then you must act, and act quickly.

The competent lifesaver follows a prescribed pattern, planning his rescue and considering his options before any action is taken. He uses the easiest, safest, fastest means at his disposal. This planning must be done quickly and calmly. The pattern to follow is called the *order of methods of rescue—reach, throw, row, go.* It starts with the easiest and most common and progresses to the more difficult.

The same progression of rescue techniques is applied in all situations. However, since people require assistance in the water under a wide variety of circumstances, the actual details will differ, depending not only on the distance from shore and the availability of equipment, but also on the condition of the water and the type of victim.

Under normal water conditions, the rescue techniques we will discuss for various types of victims present little danger to the trained rescuer. Much of the reason behind a definite progression of rescue procedures is to maximize safety. In heavy surf or a swollen river, lifesaving can become extremely hazardous, and rescues not performed from shore must be left to highly trained professionals with special equipment. The chances of you encountering such a situation are slight, but there could be a time when you must refrain from action other than going for help. Nothing is accomplished by a vain rescue attempt in which the well-intentioned rescuer becomes a victim.

Victim Recognition and Characteristics

What does a drowning person look like? The picture just formed in your mind is probably right, and at the same time, very incomplete. The first step in a rescue is recognizing the need to act. Sometimes it is obvious. A capsized canoeist might be frantically swimming for the shore while being swept toward rapids. People clinging to the top of a car swept off a high-water crossing might be shouting for help. Bystanders might be pointing to a person drifting facedown who appears unconscious. Often the situation is not so dramatic, and the need for aid is not that apparent. A child who appears to be playing might actually be in trouble. *It is important to note that a person in difficulty will not necessarily call for help and might not appear to be struggling.*

A person in peril of drowning can be classified by different schemes, including distressed or drowning, conscious or unconscious, active or passive. Categories are less important than recognizing characteristics that influence rescue procedures. Although it is acknowledged that there are no universal stereotypes for people in trouble and that victims do not always display specific behaviors, it is nevertheless useful to enumerate various types. A victim might progress from one type to another while the rescue is being undertaken.

Tired swimmer. A tired swimmer will generally ask for help. He might be swimming ineffectually in short bursts, proceeding slowly with a weak stroke, or clinging to a floating device or lifeline. He lacks, or thinks he lacks, the energy to make it to shore and simply needs a helping hand. The tired swimmer is calm, will reply to questions, and will cooperate with the assist.

Distressed swimmer. A swimmer in distress exhibits various degrees of anxiety or panic. Often he is a poor swimmer who has exceeded his capabilities. He is no longer making any progress but is still able to struggle sufficiently to keep his head out of the water most of the time. He might wave or call for help. If he were able to level off and apply the same energy to his swimming effort, he could probably reach safety on his own. He might act on clear instructions and reach for equipment as it is presented. Nonbuoyant rescue aids can probably be used. Once aid is provided, the distressed swimmer might become calm and even assist by assuming a prone position and kicking; however, the rescuer should realize that it might take a long time for the victim to return to a normal state of mind and behavior. Contact should be avoided. The longer a distressed swimmer remains in trouble, the more likely it is that he will exhibit the symptoms of the drowning nonswimmer. Timing of the rescue is therefore important, but the rescuer might have a few minutes to act.

Drowning nonswimmer. A drowning nonswimmer lacks the ability to remain at the surface and generally will submerge in less than a minute. He is unable to call or wave for help and must be recognized on the basis of his facial expression and inadequate movement. He is usually vertical in the water. Although conscious, he probably cannot respond to commands and might be unable to reach for nearby equipment. Once assisted, the drowning nonswimmer might try to remain vertical and resist horizontal tows. Contact should be avoided. Buoyant aids are needed for support. A poor swimmer in distress might progress to the "drowning nonswimmer" stage. For example, should a nonswimmer be knocked off an air mattress, he probably would be unable to reach for it and would submerge in 20 to 60 seconds without ever calling for help. Speed in rescue is essential.

Unconscious victims. Unaided, both the drowning nonswimmer and the distressed swimmer will eventually lose consciousness. Swimmers under the influence of alcohol or other drugs also might lose consciousness, often without any warning, as can victims of heart attack or stroke. An unconscious victim might float near the surface or sink. In either case, speed is of utmost necessity. Breathing has probably stopped and must be started as soon as possible if the victim is to survive. Since an unconscious victim cannot grasp an object, some type of physical contact will be required to recover him from the water.

Injured victim. The situation can be compounded if the victim is injured. Head and spinal injuries can be caused by diving into shallow water or being struck by surfboards or other objects. Cuts and broken bones can result from boat collisions, cars entering the water, or rapids. Burns can occur from gasoline explosions on motorboats. Fishermen might be entangled in hooks. In such cases, general first aid rules apply: *Treat the most serious condition first, and do no further harm.* In drowning situations, the most serious condition is likely to be lack of breathing. On the other hand, many standard rescue techniques can greatly worsen a spinal injury. We will address these concerns in a separate section.

As we proceed, we will discuss how rescue procedures are influenced by the type of victim. Those factors are often secondary to others that influence the sequence of *reach, throw, row, and go.* We will follow this sequence in the discussion, but there will be various options under each heading. Try to retain the "big picture." Some of the skills are specialized and not always appropriate. Often the best technique will require the least explanation. In an actual rescue, you will need to link various skills into a proper sequence. That task is easiest if a reaching rescue can be used.

Reaching Rescues

Reaching rescues are safe, simple, and highly effective. The poor swimmer often experiences difficulty as soon as he enters water over his head. This is likely to be close to the edge of a pool, dock, or other structure from which the victim entered the water. Well over half of all drownings occur within twenty feet of safety. If the victim is quite close, lie down and extend a hand. Nothing could be simpler. It could, however, save a life.

When you establish contact with the victim, he often will stop his own efforts to remain afloat. Such action can topple the unprepared rescuer into the water. This is the reason for lying down or otherwise bracing yourself.

If the victim is beyond the reach of your hand or leg, use any available object to extend your reach. This might be a pole, paddle, stick, or towel. Again, keep your weight low and well braced. The victim will grab for whatever object you extend. Some victims, however, might not be able to reach for an object. It must, therefore, be placed in contact with his hands. You will, of course, have to grasp an unconscious victim yourself, normally with your hand, although a special device can be found at many pools. The shepherd's crook is a pole with a large loop at one end. This loop allows an unconscious victim to be snagged just below the shoulders and drawn to shore.

The simplest reaching rescues are performed without entering the water. In some cases, however, your reach can only be extended sufficiently by going partway toward the victim. You should be firmly supported by a rigid object, such as the edge of the pool, a dock, a ladder, or the ground. An efficient technique in shallow water is the human chain, as seen in the illustration.

Reaching rescues are also used for those who have broken through the ice. First try extensions such as a ladder or plank. Lacking these, a human chain can again be used. Distribute your weight over as much area as possible.

Throwing Rescues

If a victim is beyond your reach, try a **throwing** rescue. A float with a line attached is best, but either a float or a line can be used independently. Hoses, PFDs, tires, and even wooden benches can be thrown or shoved toward a victim. Be sure to allow for wind and current, so that help will land within his reach but doesn't hit him. Keep your eye on the victim at all times.

Recoiling a line

An unweighted rope, or heaving line, should be coiled before a toss. Tie a bowline in the near end and pass a loop through it to make a running knot that will fit your wrist. Slip this loop over your nonthrowing hand to anchor the line when you throw. To coil a line for a right-handed throw, place the left hand on your left knee and stretch the line to the full reach of your right hand, then return the line from your right hand to your left hand to form your first coil. If you leave your left hand fixed to your knee and reach as far as possible each time with your right hand, all of the coils will be the same size and less likely to tangle when thrown.

Ring buoy throw

When approximately half of the line is coiled, gather the loops with your left-hand index finger and coil the rest of the line on your remaining fingers. This will allow you to separate the rope into two coils, one from which the line feeds and one that is thrown.

With one coil in each hand, throw the free coil underhand toward the victim. The rest of the line will pay off the open palm of your left hand. The line should fall over the shoulder of the victim in reach of his hands. If you miss, recoil quickly and try again. Watch the victim and not the line when recoiling. Fix your left hand firmly on your knee to avoid shaking and tangling the line when recoiling quickly.

Unweighted line throw

Throw any free-floating support.

When the victim grasps the line, grip the rope with your thumbs inward and pull in the line hand over hand. Pull fast enough to keep the victim afloat, but do not jerk the line from his hands. Words of encouragement are always appropriate.

When using the line for a whitewater rescue, the technique is slightly changed. Rather than attaching the line to your wrist, tie the line to a tree or rock with a couple of round turns and a half hitch. The force of the current on the victim might be more than you can hold alone. If no tree is handy, sit down after throwing the line and run it across your back.

33

Brace yourself securely when tending a line extended in a strong current.

Brace your feet as well as possible. It might be easier for the victim to pull himself ashore than for you to take in the slack. In deep water, allow the victim to swing across the current to the shore. Canoeists often carry rescue lines stuffed in a rescue bag, which is a small nylon tube with a weighted float at the bottom. The bag can be accurately thrown without the need for coiling rope.

A line is one of the most versatile and readily available of all rescue equipment. We will return to it later for other rescue operations. For now, practice until you can throw a coil quickly and accurately.

A ring buoy is coiled and thrown in the same fashion as a heaving line, except that now there is no need to separate the line into two coils. The buoy itself provides the weight necessary for an accurate throw. Prepare the ring buoy for use by coiling the line and holding it ready in your nonthrowing hand. Throw the buoy beyond the victim with the line falling on his shoulder. Then pull the buoy to him. An excellent makeshift buoy for a home pool or a troop swim kit can be made from a gallon plastic jug weighted with about an inch of water. Attach fifty feet of $\frac{3}{16}$-inch nylon or other light line. The jug is thrown underhand just like a regular buoy.

The ring buoy is an excellent rescue device, especially at a lake or other large swimming area. However, even the best equipment is worthless unless you can use it. Practice is again essential.

A ring buoy without a line can be thrown to a victim for support. However, your first throw must be accurate and you might need another way of bringing the victim ashore. Any other light floating object can also be used. Other PFD types are often found around the water. Cinched tight, a life jacket can be thrown easily and accurately. In an emergency, stay calm, glance around, and if the victim is beyond your reach, throw whatever is available.

Heaving line

Rescue bag

Ring buoy and flotation device

Rowing Rescues

If you see a person in distress too far from shore for a reaching or throwing rescue to be effective, use a boat if one is available. A boat is generally faster than a swimming rescue and far safer. The boat will provide complete support and will allow cardiopulmonary resuscitation (CPR) at the site if needed.

When using a rowboat, bring the boat near the victim and pivot so that he can grasp the stern. If he is strong enough to hold onto the boat, tow him to shore. If not, help him aboard over the transom. Be careful not to swamp the boat. If more than one victim is present, throw PFDs to the victims as you approach.

Two rescuers, one to row and one to watch the victim, can effect an easier rescue. The coxswain can extend a pole or extra oar to the victim as the boat approaches.

When using a canoe for the rescue, throw a PFD to the victim as you approach and then extend your paddle to him. Sit on the bottom of the boat to prevent capsizing. You can allow the victim to hold onto the stern as you paddle to shore, or, if he is tired, steady the canoe with your paddle as he climbs aboard.

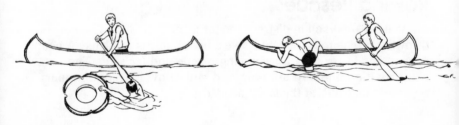

**Have passenger in boat
extend the oar.**

A motorboat should head into the wind when approaching the victim to prevent the boat from being blown over the victim. Disengage the prop as you approach and ease up to the victim. Throw a PFD as you cover the last few feet. Extend a boathook or paddle and pull the victim to the side or stern (with the motor off) where he can be helped in when calm. Watch the victim at all times as you approach. The farther the victim is from shore, the more difficult it will be to find his exact location if he submerges before you can give assistance. It is best to mark the victim's location as you approach with two objects on the far shore. If the victim submerges, watch the spot where he went down. If you become confused, you know he must be near the line defined by the two objects you chose.

The only sure way of pinpointing a location on the water is for two people to align objects with the victim from two different locations. The spot where the watchers' lines of sight cross is the location of the victim. You should serve as a second spotter if someone else has already begun a rescue effort. Pinpointing the victim's location is also the job of the lookout at a troop swim or at the camp boating area.

If the victim does submerge, you must enter the water where he was last seen and bring him back to the boat using techniques we will discuss under swimming rescues. For now, consider what will happen if you leave the boat.

In even a gentle breeze, a light boat such as a canoe will drift away faster than you can swim, especially if you have a victim in tow. The problem is made worse if you kick the boat away when entering the water. Not only will it drift faster, but you will lose your orientation if you do not recover the victim on the first dive.

The best way to overcome this difficulty is to have two rescuers in the boat. One can maintain the boat's position while also guarding the other rescuer's safety. If two rescuers are not available, an anchor will stop the boat's motion. Unfortunately, most small boats are not so equipped. Many boats, however, do have tie lines, or painters, that the rescuer can hold if the water is not too deep.

Mouth-to-mouth resuscitation must be started as soon as possible. Do not wait until you return an unconscious victim to shore. Begin at the boat. You can often support a victim adequately at the transom of a small craft. Otherwise, bring him aboard. If the victim's condition is further complicated by a lack of circulation, then a rigid support will be necessary for complete CPR. You will have to use your judgment as to the best course of action, depending on the type of boat, the number of rescuers, and the distance to shore.

Up to now it has been assumed that you know how to handle a small boat. It is an unfortunate shortcoming of most lifesaving programs, including this one, that small-boat handling is not included in the requirements. This is not because boat rescues are unimportant. Rather it is because of the amount of time necessary to become proficient maneuvering small boats, especially since different skills are required for different craft. You should not consider your lifesaving training complete until you master the craft common to your area. Such training is provided by the other aquatics merit badges. Boat rescues are explained more completely in *Canoeing, Whitewater, Rowing,* and *Small-Boat Sailing* merit badge pamphlets.

However, do not bypass the use of a boat for a rescue just because you don't know how to row or cannot yet steer a canoe by yourself. In a life-or-death situation, correct form is important only because it allows you to proceed rapidly with the least waste of energy. But if you have difficulty reaching a victim by what you think is the correct way, forget about looks. Get in the front of the boat and paddle, stroking first on one side and then the other. This will work with rowboats, canoes, small powerboats and even small sailboats if the sail is down. It will allow you to make headway in a wind when you might otherwise be blown off course. In a final effort, or if you find a boat without paddles or oars, you can enter the water and swim the boat to the victim. However, such action is really a *going* rescue rather than a *rowing* procedure. This brings us to the final step in the order of methods of rescue.

Emergency rowing—not the best way, but if it gets you to the victim, use it.

Going Rescues

A **go** rescue is a swimming rescue. It is best performed with some type of floating support and should not be considered until faster, easier, and safer rescue methods of reach, throw, and row have been attempted. Each type of rescue technique we have discussed has been more complicated and has required more skill than the last. Because of the many factors involved in a **go** rescue, we need a quick overview of items to be considered before discussing each part in detail. Those items are assessment, equipment selection, entry, approach, ready position, assist, and follow-up.

Assessment. You should have already determined the condition of the victim while looking for ways to perform the rescue from shore. Now that you are thinking about entering the water yourself, first focus your attention on the condition of the water; assess the depth, temperature, currents, and any obstacles. Don't enter the water until you have a plan that is safe for both you and the victim. Seek help from others as needed. Proceed only if you appear to be the most qualified rescuer available.

Equipment selection. A buoyant aid is superior, but any object is better than no object. We will discuss these in general and consider some special devices and techniques in detail.

Entry. The best way to enter the water depends on the water depth, the condition of the victim, and the aid being used. Bulky clothes should be removed before entering the water.

Approach. Shout encouragement to a conscious victim. Use a breaststroke or crawl modified to transport equipment, and make frequent observations of the victim. Approach a victim of possible spinal injury with extreme care.

Ready position. On arriving close to the victim (six to ten feet), stop and take a ready position. Talk to him, reevaluate the situation, and present your equipment aid.

Assist. Decide on the method that best suits your equipment, the victim, and the water conditions. Physical contact is made only if the victim is unconscious or otherwise unable to hold onto the towing aid.

Follow-up. Help the victim from the water. Secure medical aid if needed.

We'll delay further consideration of equipment selection until we get to equipment assists. We'll begin with entry into the water.

Entering the Water

An important consideration before entering the water is determining the entry point. If you can get closer to the victim sooner by running along the shoreline or edge of the pool, then do so. Take proper care not to trip or fall; you must keep watch on the victim's location. If the bank is irregular or covered by rough vegetation, then swimming from your present location might be best. The edges of lakes often have patches of weeds or submerged trees. You might have to move along the bank until you have a clear path in the water to the victim. In a river, allow for current and enter upstream of the victim.

Disrobing for rescues. A swimming rescue often requires advanced swimming ability and stamina. Swimming while supporting another person, even if you have a float on which to rest, is often exhausting, and speed is necessary if the victim is not breathing. Because of this, it would be foolish to burden yourself with unnecessary weight when covering much distance. Therefore we will learn how to remove excess clothing quickly, clothing which also can be used as

rescue equipment. The few seconds it takes to remove your clothing will be regained easily by your increased ease of swimming. The weight of wet clothing combined with the victim's weight can lead to exhaustion and an unsuccessful rescue.

You have an opportunity to practice rapid disrobing at least once a day. With a little practice you can easily disrobe in less than twenty seconds. Here's how:

Keeping your eye on the victim, remove your shoes while unfastening your belt and pants. Low shoes can be removed by stepping on the heels; you might have to stoop to remove boots or high-laced shoes. Run in place to work your pants down while removing your shirt. Hold the shirt in your teeth if it is the only equipment available. Hook a thumb in a sock at the ankle above the pants and flip the pants and sock off one foot at a time.

Beach entry. The water is often shallow at the edge of a lake, river, or ocean. If the shoreline is free of obstacles, enter at a run, lifting your legs high to avoid tripping, and holding your equipment out of the water. If your aid is large and buoyant, you might want to throw it ahead of you, provided current or waves won't sweep it away. As the water deepens, and running becomes

Beach entry

41

difficult, kick off the bottom into a shallow dive, being careful to remain near the surface, and not losing contact with your equipment. If the victim is small, don't overlook the possibility that you might be able to stand nearby and perform a reaching assist.

Ease-in entry. There are several ways to enter deep water from the edge of a pool, dock, or low bank. However, anytime you don't know the depth, or the depth is less than five feet, you should slip into the water, regardless of the condition of the victim or the type of equipment. You also should slip in if you suspect a spinal injury in order to prevent splashing and other motions that could rock the victim.

Ease-in entry

Stride jump. The stride jump or leaping entry allows you to keep the victim in sight as you enter deep water. It can be used from low heights, less than three feet, into water greater than five feet as though you were trying to land close to the victim without further

3 feet maximum

Stride jump (leaping entry)

effort. Spring outward with your body leaning slightly forward, your legs spread front and back in a scissors position, ready to snap together as they enter the water. The arms are stretched forward and outward ready to be brought down hard and fast on the surface. If you jump correctly your head will remain above the water. It might take several practice tries until you learn the proper timing for the downward thrust of the arms. Generally, if you are using a buoyant aid, you can throw it ahead of you before leaping in. However, be aware that wind, waves, or current could carry it away. If the aid is equipped with a shoulder loop, hold the float and excess line to the side as you jump and release it in midair. If you are using a garment or towel as an aid, you can loop it over your neck or grasp it with your teeth.

Feetfirst entry

Feetfirst entry. The feetfirst entry or compact jump is useful when you are wearing a PFD, when you need to maintain contact with a soft buoyant aid, or when the height is too great for a comfortable stride jump (three to five feet). It should be done only in deep water and from heights less than five feet. If you are more than five feet above the water, climb lower until you can safely enter the water.

Feetfirst entry is done in a vertical position with your legs together and knees slightly flexed. Keep your head erect and your eyes on the victim. If you have already thrown your equipment ahead of you, then your arms should be at your side. If you are wearing a PFD, fold your arms tightly across your chest and grasp the shoulders or sides of the PFD to hold it in place. If you are carrying a rescue tube or other soft, compact buoyant device, squeeze it tightly to your chest under your arms. Do not hold a rigid rescue device close to your chest when jumping from great height.

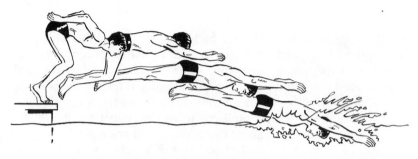

Long shallow dive

Long shallow dive. A long shallow dive is useful in deep, unobstructed water when speed is critical; for instance, after the victim has already submerged. It is not as well suited for use with equipment as the other entries discussed previously. You might remember the skill from your work for the Swimming merit badge. Begin with your feet on the edge of the deck, your knees flexed, your arms down, and your head up. Your back should be nearly parallel with the deck. Start the forward motion by swinging your arms backward and leaning forward. Then immediately swing the arms down and forward while thrusting with your legs. This will drive your body out over the water almost parallel to the surface. Drop your head slightly in flight so that you enter the water at a slight angle. (No belly flops, please!) Keep your arms extended and your toes pointed until your glide starts to slow down. Then begin swimming.

The Approach

The approach path will generally be in a direct line to the victim. Although some assists might eventually be from the rear or the side, the initial approach should normally place you facing the victim. Frequent visual observation must be maintained, and verbal communication and encouragement should be part of every approach to a conscious victim.

The rescuer should adapt his swimming stroke to the condition of the victim, the condition of the water, the type of aid being carried, and the distance. A crawl is the fastest stroke, and speed is critical for an unconscious victim. Speed is increased if you swim with your face in the water; however, you should occasionally glance forward as you breathe to refocus on the victim. A breaststroke might be more efficient in rough water. If there are obstacles in the water (rocks, trees, weeds), then you need to swim with your head up to avoid them.

A buoyant aid is most easily towed with a line. Special rescue aids have shoulder loops that allow the rescuer to swim using a crawl stroke with the float trailing behind. However, such aids are generally available only where lifeguards are present; the lifesaver might need to adapt to other situations. For example, the best way to transport a PFD to a victim might be for the rescuer to wear it during the approach. That would allow a crawl stroke to be used. A second PFD could be transported using a head-up breaststroke with the strap held in the rescuer's teeth or looped over an arm.

Buoyant aids without straps or lines can be pushed ahead of a rescuer using a breaststroke, or, if necessary, towed using a sidestroke. Large objects such as surfboards, air mattresses, or larger inner tubes can be ridden and propelled with the arms.

A garment or towel can be draped across the neck for the crawl or grasped by the teeth in a head-up breaststroke. If the aid is nonbuoyant and the victim goes under and remains submerged during the approach, then the aid is no longer useful and may be dropped.

At times the details of the approach stroke will be unimportant; for example, many backyard, apartment, and hotel pools are so small that the approach and entry are simultaneous. On the other hand, a large distance to cover in open water might dictate that you use a paced approach to conserve energy needed for the assist. Flexibility, common sense, due caution, and training are more critical than hard and fast rules.

Ready Position

Before you make a final approach to assist the victim, you should stop well out of reach, prepare to reverse direction, speak to the victim, and reevaluate the situation.

We have been building a **go** rescue in a series of steps. At each stage, different choices have been available. Decisions you made earlier will influence your options now, but you might still have important choices to make depending on the condition of the victim (responsive or uncooperative, conscious or unconscious, floating or submerged, spinal injury indicated or not) and the equipment available or lacking.

Many items near the water can serve as floating support.

Equipment Assists

Any object that floats well enough to support your weight and is light enough for you to move through the water can be used in a **go** rescue. Inner tubes, PFDs, air mattresses, or inflated tires can all be used in an emergency. Push or pull the object to the victim.

When close to a conscious victim, stop and extend the device for him to grab. Talk to him and explain clearly what you want him to do. Some victims will be unable to reach for an object even though they see it and it is only inches away. You might have to shove the aid into direct contact with the victim's arms or hands. When he is calm, tow both him and the device ashore. Normally, the rescuer will be ahead of the victim with the buoyant aid between, and will use a sidestroke for the tow. If the buoyant device is small and awkward, it might be better to allow the victim to hold it to his chest while you swim at his side holding his armpit. Continue to reassure him during the tow.

If the victim is unconscious, the situation is more difficult and the need for speed more important since it is likely he is not breathing.

Push flotation support to the victim.

If you are only a few feet from safety, such as in a backyard pool, you might elect to abandon your float and tow him quickly to shallow water or the side. If a longer distance is involved, and particularly if the victim is heavy, try to use the float to support either yourself or the victim, but make sure his face remains clear of the water. If your equipment is a wearable PFD, it makes sense for you to have it on.

Rescue board. The rescue board is an excellent device in trained hands. The rescuer who is proficient in its use can slice through waves easier than a swimmer. The board also allows a rapid approach on calm water. We will consider only the most elementary use of this aid. Although a proper rescue board is a special device, similar techniques can be used with recreational surfboards, bodyboards, or sailboards (preferably without the mast attached).

Lie on the board with your head up. Use your arms in breast-stroke fashion to propel a rescue board, surfboard, or sailboard. If you are using fins with a bodyboard, a kick will be more efficient. When close to a conscious victim, slip off the board and push it side-ways to him, with the board between the two of you. If the victim has trouble holding on, you can grasp his wrists across the board. You can push the board to shore with the victim holding onto the side, or if he is calm, you can have him lie facedown on the board.

If it is necessary to place the victim on the board and he is unable to get on by himself, turn the board over and pull his arms across it.

Hold his arms in place with one hand, grasp the opposite edge with the other, and roll him onto the board by flipping it toward you. Keep the bow pointed toward shore if there are waves.

Paddle to victim.

Grab victim's wrist and slide off board.

Place board between victim and rescuer.

Roll board over.

Position victim.

Paddle to shore.

Rescue buoy. A rescue buoy is a highly buoyant rigid-plastic float with molded handles and a towline with a shoulder loop attached. It is primarily designed for surf rescue but can be used in any body of water. It is towed behind the rescuer during the approach, presented to the victim who is allowed to grasp the handles, and then towed in. Other types of buoys might have an additional line attached that is fed from a reel on the shore. However, these devices are normally available only to trained rescue teams.

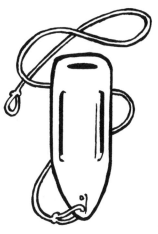

Rescue buoy

Rescue tube. The rescue tube is similar in concept to the rescue buoy, but it's made of flexible vinyl-covered foam. It is a bit less buoyant than a rescue buoy, but is generally easier to use. It also has a shoulder loop attached which allows the tube to be towed behind the rescuer on approach who, as before, extends the float to a conscious victim and then tows him in. If the victim is unconscious, the tube can be snapped around the victim's body under the shoulders.

Rescue tube

The rescue tube is probably the best rescue device available for swimmer protection at a pool. (A reach pole is a close competitor.) When flat, the rescue tube can be used for reaching rescues, and, with the ends fastened together to form a ring, it is even useful for short throwing rescues. Although expensive, it should be considered for the troop swim kit.

You should remember that a lifeline was suggested for lifeguard use under the Safe Swim Defense plan. A rescue tube is equipped with a ring on one end to which that line can be attached. This allows a second rescuer on shore to pull in both the victim and the swimming rescuer.

Line tender rescue. Rescue tubes often are not available for troop swim protection. Rope by itself however is easily obtained and should be a standard item on troop outings. In cases where a line cannot be thrown, either because of distance or difficulties with intervening swimmers, the line can be taken to the victim by a swimmer. The rescuer should of course also carry some type of floating device, such as a PFD.

Place bowline over shoulder and under opposite arm of the swimming rescuer.

A large bowline in the end of the line is placed over the shoulder and under the opposite arm of the swimming rescuer. The swimmer pulls out the line, presents his floating object to a conscious victim, and when ready, signals for the line tender to pull them to safety using a hand-over-hand motion. If a floating aid is not available, the swimmer moves to the side and just beyond the victim, then turns so that the line is pulled into the victim's reach. If the victim cannot grasp the float or the line, then the swimming rescuer

Line tender feeds out line to avoid tangling as rescuer goes to victim.

Line tender pulls in rescuer and victim hand over hand, grasping line with thumbs in.

should grasp the victim and hold his head out of the water as the line tender pulls them in.

It is the line tender's responsibility to prevent the line from fouling as the swimmer moves toward the victim. The line can be held in a simple coil anchored to the tender's wrist by a running loop. The coil must be completely free of tangles, and should be recoiled whenever guards are changed and whenever the line is laid down for any reason. It is often necessary to wet and stretch newly laid (three-strand twisted) rope to prevent the coils from assuming figure-eight patterns. Braided rope will not have the same twisting problems. Braided polypropylene is good because it floats, but line from this material is best if it has a solid core rather than the hollow, loose weave of waterskiing rope. The line should be of small diameter and long enough to cover the swimming area.

There are two other ways of storing the line, both of which make it easier to hold and keep it free from tangles. One is to use a rescue

Line tender rescue

If there is no floating aid, rescuer swims past victim, putting the line in his reach. Line tender pulls them both to safety.

If the victim can't grasp, the rescuer holds the victim's head out of water as line tender pulls them in.

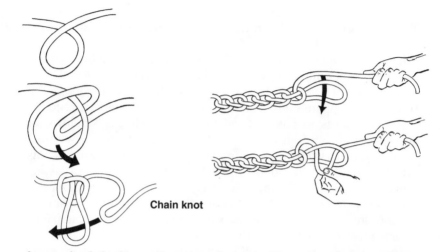

Chain knot

bag to feed the line rather than throw it. The other is a chain knot, which is a series of interlocked slipknots that shortens the apparent length of the line, as seen in the illustration. The line tender pulls the line free from the chain knot as the rescue swimmer approaches the victim.

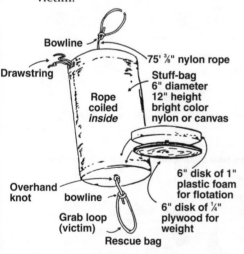

Bowline

Drawstring

75' ⅜" nylon rope

Stuff-bag
6" diameter
12" height
bright color
nylon or canvas

Rope coiled *inside*

Overhand knot   bowline

6" disk of 1" plastic foam for flotation

Grab loop (victim)

6" disk of ¼" plywood for weight

Rescue bag

Shirttail rescue. A **go** rescue with a floating device is preferred if a swimming assist must be made. Both victim and rescuer can use it as support. An extra margin of safety is added if a line is attached to the float or rescuer and tended by a second lifesaver. Sometimes, however, a floating object cannot be found. Your next option is to carry anything that can be extended to the victim even if it is not sufficient to keep him afloat. This might be a shirt, towel, short rope, pole, or paddle. The extension will separate you from the victim and make it easier to swim. You will have to swim fast enough to keep the victim's head above water.

Shirttail rescue

This is easier if you can talk him into turning onto his back. You will have to give clear instructions to the victim when you extend your object and as you begin the tow.

If the victim tries to climb along the extension to grasp you directly, then let go. Reverse away, reassure him, and resume the tow only when he has calmed down.

Assists Without Equipment

Think for a moment, seriously. Can you imagine any realistic situation in which you would be forced to enter the water to aid a struggling victim with no equipment available? No shirt, no towel, no anything? Hard to imagine, isn't it? There is always something around if you will take a few seconds to go after it, and of course there is never an excuse for anyone who calls himself a lifeguard to be without rescue equipment. Rescues involving physical contact with a conscious victim are seldom really necessary. Not only that, it can further endanger the victim because it can place the rescuer himself at risk. There are only a few situations when a contact rescue should be considered:

- A calm person asks for assistance due to fatigue, cramps, or another problem. This is really just a "tired swimmer" rather than a victim requiring rescue. If you have to enter the water to help such a person, you should take a buoyant aid with you. But if you are already in the water, swimming to shore to get an aid might cause sufficient delay for the person to get into real trouble. In such a case you can safely offer assistance without equipment.

- There really is no equipment at hand. This would indicate that a rescuer wearing little clothing is already in the water a considerable distance from safety when he becomes aware of a nearby victim. This could be the result of an uncommon accident such as a fall from a bridge or the deck of a ship. Even so, it might still be possible to lead the victim to safety without contact.

- It is possible that some victims under duress, although obviously conscious and uninjured, will be unable to grasp or maintain a grip on a piece of equipment, particularly if it is nonbuoyant, such as a shirt.

- When a victim has lost consciousness, the risk to the rescuer is reduced, but more importantly, some amount of physical contact will be necessary to move the victim to a place where resuscitation can be performed.

- The victim of a spinal injury might be conscious or not, but will always require an elaborate procedure involving physical contact to be safely removed from the water.

We will consider each of these cases in turn. However, the techniques for dealing with spinal injury are specialized and will be discussed in a separate section.

Tired-swimmer assist. Often a tired swimmer only needs a bit of encouragement and coaxing. If physical assistance is needed, a simple technique, called an *underarm swim-along*, is to push the swimmer forward as he swims on his own by placing one hand under his armpit with your thumb up and swimming alongside and slightly to the rear. The victim can be swimming either on his front or back. If a second person is available to help, he can push holding beneath the other arm. Again, the victim can be either on his front or back, but a back float position is more restful for him if a long distance is to be covered. In either case, give the victim clear instructions and maintain conversation to keep him alert and cooperative.

Talk and lead. If you are faced with a panicked victim without any equipment available, then first try to talk the victim in. If the victim can keep his head above water, then he can swim; he just isn't making the right motions. Tell him to level off and kick toward you. If he does not obey your instructions, he might at least move in the direction of your voice. If he does, back up toward shore. Encourage this action; tell him to come to you so that you can help. Little by little you might be able to lead him into shallow water. This might seem like callous trickery, but it is better than risking both of your lives trying to overcome someone controlled by fear. If an active victim will not follow you to shore, back off and wait. He might become

Underarm swim-along

Two-person assist

more cooperative as he becomes exhausted. As long as the victim can keep his head above water, and if the water is warm and you are not being carried toward danger by currents, you are not forced to act. You are close enough to place the victim in a tow if it becomes necessary. Remember, however, that we are now discussing extremely rare situations; almost always a simpler means of rescue is available.

Talk and lead

Tows and carries for a conscious victim. If you have been forced to wait for a struggling victim to become exhausted or if a drowning nonswimmer will not grab the equipment you have brought along, then physical contact can no longer be avoided. This is an exercise in good judgment. It is obvious that you should not make contact with a violently thrashing victim, but that is really not a common drowning response. Often the victim will be about to submerge by the time you reach him. Nevertheless, when you approach a conscious victim without equipment, you should first approach from the front and try to get the victim to respond to your commands. Once it is clear that the victim will not long remain on the surface without help, then swim behind him. (If he follows you around, let him follow you to shore.) You will then be in position for a contact assist. However, do not make contact with a conscious victim without giving a verbal warning.

Single armpit tow. Once you are behind the victim, tuck your legs under your body and lean away from him. Close the remaining gap by paddling with your hands. This *ready position* places you in a good swimming position before contact and prepares you to support the victim with your kick. Tell him to lean back and relax. Reach out with your hand nearest him and grasp under his armpit with your thumb up and on the outside. (Your right hand goes to the right armpit, or your left hand to the left armpit.) Immediately begin swimming to keep the victim's face above water. Use whatever kick gives you the most power. If the victim thrashes and breaks your grip, back off, reevaluate, and try again. Don't try to overpower a victim; it is unnecessary, risky, and wastes energy you will need for the tow.

Single armpit tow

Cross-chest carry. If you have difficulty maintaining control of the victim's position and keeping his face clear of the water with the armpit tow, you can use the cross-chest carry. This might be the case if the water is choppy or if the victim fidgets. However, be aware that the cross-chest carry is more tiring for the rescuer. After getting under way with the armpit tow, which should help to bring the victim to a horizontal position, bring your free arm over the corresponding shoulder of the victim and across his chest until your hand is in contact with the victim's side just below his armpit. Hold him firmly against the side of your chest, with your hip in the middle of his back. You can use either a regular or an inverted scissors kick. Make sure you keep the victim's face above water. This position might be slightly more reassuring for the victim than the armpit tow, but keep in mind that neither is particularly natural or comfortable. Continue to offer verbal assurances. Depending on the water conditions and the relative sizes of the victim and the rescuer, the rescuer might choose to go directly into the cross-chest carry without first using the armpit tow. If a breaking wave or other disturbance causes the victim to lurch, you can easily maintain your grip with the cross-chest carry. However, if he doesn't rapidly

settle down but rather begins to thrash about, you may decide to let go, wait for him to tire, and start over.

Tows and carries for an unconscious victim. Both the single armpit tow and the cross-chest carry can be used for an unconscious victim. However, there are other techniques for use only on unconscious victims that might be easier and quicker. Remember that speed is essential for a victim who might not be breathing.

Wrist tow. Approach the victim from the front and assume the ready position. Shout and splash water at him to make sure he is unconscious. Then come within an arm's length, reach across to the victim's opposite wrist as if you were shaking hands, and take hold under his wrist with your palm up. Hold firmly and roll your wrist by turning your thumb up and over as you begin your tow. This will turn the victim onto his back. Maintain the same grip as you tow the victim to safety with a sidestroke. A slight tension in your arm is necessary to keep the victim's face up. Both your arm and the victim's arm should remain straight.

The wrist tow is easy to perform on a relaxed person during practice. The victim floats on the surface and there is no interference with your kick. Minor changes in the twist of your wrist will keep his face above water. However, you should be aware of two ways a real victim can differ from a practice victim. If the victim is recovered from the bottom, he will no longer float because his lungs are not inflated. You will need a strong, fast stroke to keep him in a towing position. Also, unlike a practice victim, an unconscious victim cannot support his own head. Depending on body build and weight, you might find it difficult to keep the face of a larger unconscious victim above water with the wrist tow, particularly if the water is rough. If so, you will need to switch to another method. However, try the wrist tow first. Chances are it will work and even if it doesn't, it will place the victim in a level position for other tows. Practice the technique until you have no difficulty controlling the movements of the practice victim.

Changing from wrist tow to armpit tow. To change from a wrist tow to an armpit tow, continue kicking vigorously to maintain forward motion. Pull the victim toward you by bending your towing arm and

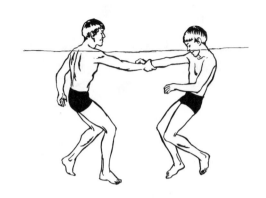

Wrist tow

using your free hand to grasp him under his other armpit. When you have a firm grip, release the victim's wrist and continue with the armpit tow.

Change from wrist tow to armpit tow.

Collar tow. Yet another technique can be used on an unconscious victim who is wearing a shirt or jacket. Grasp the collar with your palm down. Keep your towing arm straight and use it to support the victim's head. Be careful to keep his face out of the water and do not pull the clothing so tightly that you interfere with his breathing.

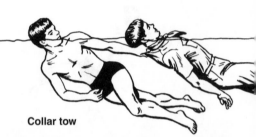

Collar tow

Submerged victim. An unconscious victim can come to rest anywhere between the surface and the bottom. If the victim is floating just below the surface, you can reach down and use the wrist tow to bring him up and forward. If the victim is deeper, you will have to use a surface dive to get close enough to bring him up. Grasp the submerged victim in any logical manner, either by his wrist, under one arm, or under both arms. If the bottom is hard and clear, you can kick against it to help you up. If the bottom is muddy or covered with weeds, it will be better to grasp the victim from above with only one hand and to use the other hand and a strong kick to pull him up. We will discuss surface dives and underwater search techniques later.

Defenses and Escapes

If you approach a victim properly while attempting a swimming rescue, it should not be necessary for you to struggle or grapple with him. But you should be familiar with some of the defenses against grasps in case you ever do need to use them, either because you made a mistake or are thrown into the water with a person who panics. If you remain calm, you easily can free yourself from any hold the victim might use.

A drowning victim wants support to keep his head clear of the water so that he can breathe. It is not his intention to hold you beneath the water. So, if you deliberately go underwater feetfirst toward the bottom at first contact, the victim probably will let go since he wanted to go up, not down. He certainly will not swim down after you. Your first defense, therefore, is to go under, fast.

Block. If the victim is extremely close and catches you by surprise, it might be necessary for you to block his forward motion by extending an arm, palm out, toward his chest. This will probably allow you to submerge free from his grasp. If he does manage to grab you, it will most likely be your blocking arm that he clasps.

Block and escape

Wrist escape. A grip on the wrist is easily broken by pulling against the victim's thumb. If possible, push the victim down as you do so. This will encourage him to let go on his own.

Rear head-hold escape. If a victim unexpectedly grabs your head from the rear, take a quick breath, tuck your chin to the side, and submerge both yourself and the victim. Then grasp the victim just above each elbow and shove upward. Be sure to keep your head

Rear head-hold escape

tucked. Swim clear of the victim before resurfacing. Do not struggle with him or try to place him in a hold. Back off and start over.

Front head-hold escape. The same technique is used if the hold is from the front. Take a quick breath, tuck your chin to the side, and submerge. Then push upward with your hands beneath his arms. Swim clear of the victim before resurfacing. Do not struggle with him or try to place him in a hold. Back off and start over.

Front head-hold escape

Surface Dives

If the victim submerges before you will be able to follow using the surface dives learned for the Swimming merit badge. Study the illustrations if you need to review these skills.

Feetfirst surface dive. This surface dive should be used if the water is murky and possibly obstructed. Lift your trunk as high as possible by pushing down with your arms and kicking upward with a scissors kick. Then straighten your legs and push your hands upward against the water to force yourself down. Do not recover the arms too quickly; they must push against the water and not the air.

Headfirst surface dive or pike surface dive. This surface dive is most easily done while moving forward with a breaststroke. As you begin a new arm stroke, bend at the waist, then reverse the direction of your stroke, pushing

Feetfirst surface dive

against the water as you lift your legs into the air. Extend your arms toward the bottom as the weight of your legs drives you downward.

Search for objects on the bottom with your eyes open. Mud stirred up by hitting the bottom will reduce your visibility quickly; therefore, avoid the bottom until the victim is found.

The depth at which you can successfully recover a submerged victim will depend on three things: how well you perform your surface dive; how long you can safely hold your breath; and how easily your ears equalize under pressure. Recall that we set the maximum depth for a safe swimming area at 12 feet.

Just because you can swim 40 feet underwater across a pool does not mean you will be able to swim 20 feet straight down. Your body's buoyancy works against you in reaching the bottom. Correct surface dives are essential. If you try to swim downward with your hands, you waste time and energy, both of which take their toll on your breath. Practice your surface dives for maximum efficiency. You should be able to reach the bottom in 8 feet of water without any underwater strokes.

Take only one or two deep breaths before diving. Breathing too deeply for too long, called hyperventilation, will result in a temporary chemical imbalance in your blood that can delay the breathing reflex and cause you to black out.

You probably have noticed a slight pain in your ears when swimming at the bottom of an 8- to 10-foot pool. The pain might have disappeared if you swallowed or wiggled your jaw. The pain is caused by the increased pressure of the water on your eardrum. If air is free to travel from your lungs to your inner ear, then the pressure is the same on each side and you feel no pain. Some people equalize automatically; others, especially if suffering from a cold, cannot equalize at all. If you are trying to recover a victim in deep water, you must return to the surface if the pain in your ears becomes intense, even if the victim is in sight. If you ignore the pain, your eardrum might rupture.

Headfirst surface dive

This will cause disorientation and possibly loss of consciousness. Then there would be two people to rescue rather than one.

If the water is deep you might be forced to wait for help from someone with more experience or special equipment. Never use weights to take you to the bottom unless you have been trained in their use.

Lost Swimmer Search

You might arrive at the scene of a presumed drowning after the victim has disappeared. Witnesses might have only a vague idea of his whereabouts. They might not even be sure he is in the water.

If the water is clear, you can search the area from the surface. However, if the bottom cannot be seen, then do not attempt an underwater search alone. Your chances of finding the victim are slim and there is no one to aid you if you encounter difficulty on the bottom. Instead, organize other swimmers into a lost swimmer search (also called LBD or lost bather drill).

In shallow water, have everyone link arms and wade in a line across the area, shuffling their feet from side to side. It should be easy to get cooperation, even from bystanders, for this type of search.

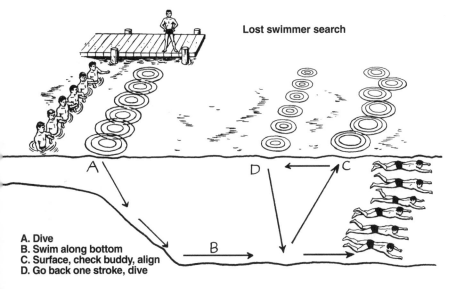

Lost swimmer search

A. Dive
B. Swim along bottom
C. Surface, check buddy, align
D. Go back one stroke, dive

In deep water, swimmers form a line, surface dive on signal from a leader, and swim a prescribed number of strokes along the bottom— three in shallow water and two in deep water. The swimmers should be paired as buddies so that anyone failing to return to the surface is instantly spotted. When everyone has surfaced, the line reforms on the person farthest behind. Then the entire line backs up a few additional feet. This is to cover any area missed because of angled surface dives. The line must reform after each dive; otherwise swimmers will begin to swim in front of each other and part of the bottom will not be covered. If a sweep of the area fails to find the victim, the search should be repeated at right angles to the previous path.

A lost swimmer search must proceed quickly and orderly with no unnecessary talking. A single leader is essential, preferably not in the water, as well as guards for the searchers. It would be difficult to organize such a search quickly and safely using people unfamiliar with the concept. The technique is practical at the troop swim site only if several swimmers have been trained in the procedure. Your troop has an opportunity to practice every time an area is searched for hazards before a swim. The instant it is suspected that a swimmer is missing, a *lost swimmer search* must be started.

Mask, Fins, and Snorkel

The ease with which you can make a search for a lost swimmer, either by yourself from the surface or underwater with a buddy, greatly increases if you are equipped with mask, fins, and snorkel. The mask improves your vision, the snorkel allows you to breathe at the surface while watching the bottom, and fins increase the distance you travel with each stroke.

The faceplate of a quality mask is of tempered glass, held in place by a ring of hard plastic or stainless steel. The rubber edges of the mask should be soft and flexible, conforming to the contours of your face. To check the fit, put the mask in place without the strap and inhale gently through your nose. The mask should remain in place when you remove your hand. The strap should be easily adjustable and split into two parts.

To use the mask, spread saliva on the inside of the faceplate and rinse once before donning. This will keep the mask from fogging. If the mask leaks or is knocked loose while swimming, press the top of the mask against the forehead in an upright position and exhale through the nose. This will force the water out the bottom of the mask as air collects in the top. The mask can also be cleared from the side by holding the upper edge and allowing the air to escape around the lower strap fitting. With practice, this skill will become automatic. If you have trouble, you can always surface and reposition the mask. However, before you use the mask as an underwater search device, you should be familiar enough with its use that a flooded mask does not cause concern. Some masks have special purge valves that make clearing easier.

We spoke earlier of equalizing the pressure in your ears and mentioned that swallowing or moving your jaw might relieve the pressure when diving. Another way is to hold your nose and blow gently. You can try it now if you wish to get the proper feel. Pinch your nostrils and try to exhale very slowly through your nose. If your eustachian tubes are clear, your ears should feel stuffy. You have perhaps experienced this feeling in a car on a steep grade or in an airplane. Do not force the maneuver—serious damage to your ears can result. The technique will not work if you have a cold or sinus problems. You can perform this same exercise before a series of surface dives to flex the eustachian tubes and make it easier to adjust to pressure underwater. A good mask will have either finger indentations or a soft pad for holding the nose shut while equalizing the ears.

The snorkel is a J-shaped tube used for breathing at the surface in a facedown position. For skin diving, the simpler the construction the better. It should have a fairly large bore and a small rubber device, or keeper, for attaching to the mask strap. There are many types of mouthpieces; choose one that is comfortable.

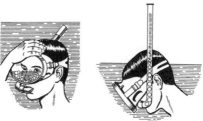

The mask and snorkel are cleared by replacing water with air.

When you submerge, the snorkel naturally will fill with water and must be cleared before you can again breathe through it. Clear the snorkel by exhaling explosively when the back of your head breaks the surface. Then cautiously inhale your next breath.

Fins come in a variety of sizes, shapes, and styles, each claiming advantages over the others. Choose a pair that fits. The blades should be slightly flexible and of medium size. Some fins float, others sink. Put the fins on while wet and only when you are ready to use them. Fins are designed for swimming, not for walking. Use a slow, wide flutter kick while swimming.

After practicing with mask, fins, and snorkel in a pool, wash them with mild soap and rinse in clean water. Store them out of the sun. Excess chlorine and sunlight can damage the material. Do not practice in open water without a float on which to rest and a flag to keep boats away. Of course, always practice with a buddy.

Mask, fins, and snorkel are important tools for the lifesaver. However, the discussion given here is rudimentary. Practice under a qualified instructor is recommended, even for the basic skills outlined above. We have discussed these items in the context of rescue equipment. Skin diving is properly a separate sport with several devices we have not discussed, including standard safety features. You might be interested in earning the Snorkeling, BSA award. This will improve your ability to use mask, fins, and snorkel, both as rescue equipment and for recreation. You will learn, for instance, better ways to clear the snorkel.

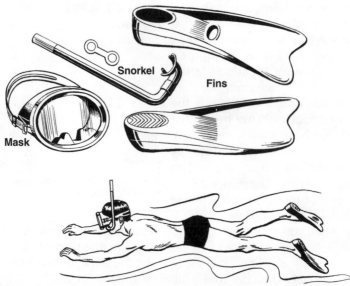

Snorkel

Fins

Mask

With fins, swim only with your legs using a slow, wide flutter kick. Keep your hands in front if the water is not clear. Swim near enough to the bottom to see the subject. If necessary feel the bottom with your hands.

Follow-up Procedure

A rescue is not complete until the victim is ashore and recovered. In many cases, the victim will be able to help himself out of the water, and your task is done when you see him warm, free from shock, and secure in the care of family or friends. However, if the victim is not breathing when you reach shore, then your actions are still critical. Artificial respiration must be started as soon as possible and the pulse must be checked for heart action. This is normally difficult in the water, and since the victim will be unable to help himself, we need to discuss ways for you to get him out of the water.

Hopefully, other people will have responded to the shouts and directions you gave before entering the water. If the victim was conscious when you began, bystanders might not have called for emergency medical assistance. You should repeat such commands while bringing the victim in. If emergency medical assistance has arrived, you can turn the situation over to them as soon as you reach shore. If advanced first aid is not available, get whatever help you can to remove the victim from the water and begin cardiopulmonary resuscitation immediately. Continue until help arrives or the victim begins breathing on his own.

Even though the victim might begin breathing again, the danger has not passed. Treat for shock and try to insist that the victim get immediate medical help. Near-drowning victims who have aspirated water (that is, breathed a small amount of water into their lungs) might collapse again after they appear recovered and can develop pneumonia.

Care should be used not to injure either the victim or yourself when removing him from the water. The following techniques are not to be used if spinal injury is suspected.

Shallow-water assist. A conscious victim can be helped from shallow water with this method. Help the victim to stand and to place one of his arms across your shoulder. Grasp the wrist

Shallow-water assist

of that arm with one hand, and wrap your free arm around his back. Then walk slowly to shore. A second person can assist from the victim's other side.

Beach drag. A drag is the easiest and safest way to remove an unconscious victim when there is a sloping bottom. Grasp the victim under his armpits and pull him onto the beach by slowly walking backward. Support his head with your forearms and keep your

Beach drag

back as straight as possible. This technique will only get the victim just past the water's edge, but that is normally sufficient to begin resuscitation if needed.

Pack-strap carry. This carry can be used for either a conscious or an unconscious victim in shallow water, but might be difficult if the victim is large. While the water is still waist deep, float the victim on his back to your side. Support him with your knee and take hold of his right wrist with your right hand and his left wrist with your left hand, with your thumbs pointing toward his shoulders. Turn your back to the victim, crouch slightly, and bring his arms over your shoulders. Cross the victim's wrists and hold them in front of your chest. His arms should be straight with the armpits directly over your shoulders. Balance the victim before you lift and while carrying him to the shore. Lower him to the ground by slowly kneeling on first one knee and then the other. Gently roll the victim to one side and lower him to the ground, taking care to protect his head.

Pack-strap carry

Vertical lift. This technique is used for unconscious victims at the edge of a pool, float, or pier. Place the victim's hands one on top of the other on the edge while keeping his head clear of the water. With one hand holding both of his on the edge, use your free hand to boost yourself out of the water. Grasp the victim's wrists and stand up near the edge directly over him. Pull him up, carefully folding him over the edge. It might be necessary to gently bob the victim up and down in the water, lifting him clear on the up stroke. Use your arms and legs rather than your back to lift. Your leg should cushion his head while you lower his trunk to the deck. Then reach down and swing his legs over the edge. Take care not to twist the victim's back. Great care must be taken to prevent injury to the victim.

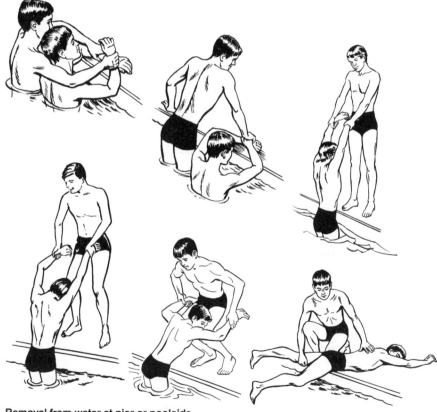

Removal from water at pier or poolside

Spinal Injury Management

Swimming injuries can often be blamed on diving into shallow or otherwise obstructed water. Even when drowning is avoided, crippling neck and back injuries can result. Studies have shown that most serious diving injuries occur to males, ages 12 to 31, diving from low heights such as the edge of a pool deck, a dock, or a pier, into water less than 5 feet deep. A spinal injury can occur when the victim's head hits the bottom or side of the pool or some other object, such as another swimmer. Spinal injuries most often happen at the shallow end of the pool, in a corner of the pool, or where the bottom drops off to deeper water. Therefore, Safe Swim Defense requires a minimum of 7 feet of water beneath and behind the point of entry for diving from the edge of a pool, pier, or floating platform. Even sufficient depth and elimination of rocks, stumps, and other obstructions are not adequate if diving is not regulated to avoid body collision.

In deciding if the spinal cord might have been injured you should consider the cause of the accident. Any fall from a height greater than the victim's height, any person found unconscious for unknown reasons, any significant head trauma, and any diving accident can indicate a spinal cord injury.

Whether the victim is conscious or unconscious, the following signs can indicate a spinal injury: pain at the fracture site, loss of movement in the extremities or below the fracture site, tingling or loss of sensation in the extremities, disorientation, back or neck deformity, visible bruising over an area of spinal column, impaired or stopped breathing, head injury, and fluid/blood in the ears.

Great care must be taken if a spinal injury is suspected. If the victim is not handled properly additional serious injury could result. Moving of the victim is an extremely delicate operation and is best left to trained personnel. However, you can not leave the victim floating facedown because of the possibility of death by drowning. If no one else is present to take charge you will need to take proper action. Proper management of the airway must be maintained at all times.

The *American Red Cross Emergency Water Safety* and *Lifeguarding* manuals are excellent resources for understanding the principles and procedures for handling a victim who is suspected of having a spinal injury.

Rescue Procedures

Carefully approach the victim so that you do not cause additional injury. Ease into the water. It is necessary to minimize the movement of the victim's head, neck, and back. The method used to limit this movement is called *in-line stabilization*. The method you use will depend on a number of factors, including the size of the victim, the rescuer's size and strength, and the buoyancy of the rescuer and the victim. You must evaluate the situation and quickly develop a plan of action.

Hip and Shoulder Support

If the victim is faceup and no help is immediately available to assist in placing the victim on a rescue board, you should support the victim at the hips and shoulders. This technique is used in calm shallow water only:

- Stand facing the victim's side, and lower yourself to chest depth.

- Slide one arm under the victim's shoulders and the other under his hip bones, and support the victim, keeping his face clear of the water for breathing.

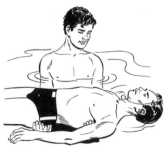

- Do not lift him, but keep him in a horizontal position in the water until help arrives.

- Comfort and reassure the victim.

Hip and shoulder support

Head/Chin Support

This technique for immobilizing the spine is called head/chin support. This technique can be used on both faceup and facedown victims:

- Approach the victim from either side.

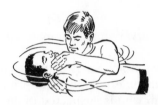

- Lower your body until your shoulders are at water level.

- Place your forearms along the length of the victim's breastbone and spine. Based on the size of the victim, you can position your top arm on the breastbone by reaching either over or under the victim's nearer arm. Place your thumb on one side of the victim's chin and your fingers on the other side. Do not apply pressure yet.

- At the same time, use your other hand to support the victim's head by spreading the fingers and cradling the head. Do not apply pressure yet.

- Lock both of your wrists and squeeze your forearms together, clamping the victim's chest and back between them. Apply gentle pressure to the chin and the back of the head. You are now providing in-line stabilization.

- Glide the victim in a horizontal position.

- If the victim is facedown, turn the victim faceup. To do this, keep your hands in position under the victim's chin and at the back of the victim's head, supporting the head. Rotate the victim toward you while you begin to submerge yourself. Carefully roll under the victim while turning the victim over in the water. The victim is faceup when you surface on the other side. This movement must be done slowly to avoid any twisting of the victim's body.

- Keep the victim in a horizontal position in the water until help arrives.

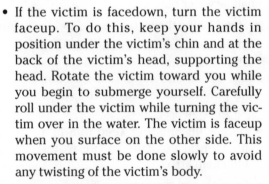

Securing the Victim to the Rescue Board

After you have stabilized the victim you are ready to secure him to the rescue board. Provide direction to other people assisting you, directing them to do the following:

- Bring the rescue board into the water and approach the victim from the side.

- Place the rescue board diagonally under the victim from the side, with the foot end of the board going down in the water first.

- Hold the board down under the water so it doesn't bump against the victim, slide it under him, and position it lengthwise along his spine. Make sure the board is beyond the victim's head near the rescuer who is maintaining in-line stabilization.

- Allow the board to rise under the victim. At least one assistant should be along each side of the board, one at the victim's feet, and two stabilizing the victim's head.

- The first rescuer stabilizing the victim's head and neck should slowly and carefully withdraw his or her arms from the top and bottom of the victim's head as the board is raised into place against the victim. A second rescuer continues to hold the victim's head steady with hands on each side of his head until the cervical collar and padding are in place.

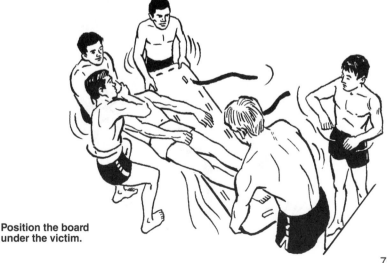

Position the board under the victim.

- After the board is in place, carefully apply an appropriately sized rigid cervical collar, while a second rescuer maintains in-line stabilization. The cervical collar should fit securely with the chin in the proper resting position and the head maintained in the neutral position by the collar.

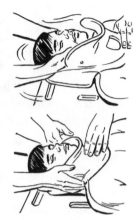

- After the cervical collar is in place, secure the victim to the rescue board using nylon straps. Begin by securing the victim's shoulders by crisscrossing the chest and securing at the sides. The straps should be snug, but not so tight as to restrict movement of the chest during normal breathing.

Apply cervical collar to victim.

- Secure the strap across the hip bones.

- Secure the hands alongside or in front of the victim.

- Secure the thighs and shins to the rescue board. If additional support is needed, put a figure-eight tie on the ankles so that the feet do not move.

Secure the victim to the rescue board.

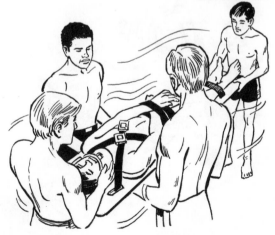

- Secure the head. Before securing the head to the board, it might be necessary to place padding, such as a folded towel, under the victim's head. The amount of padding needed will be evident from the space between the board and the head, while in-line stabilization is maintained. Normally, approximately one inch is all that is needed to keep the head in a neutral position and provide comfort for the victim.

- Continue to secure the head by placing a towel or blanket roll in a horseshoe configuration around the head and neck of the victim.

- Secure the forehead with Velcro straps, cravats, or other similar material.

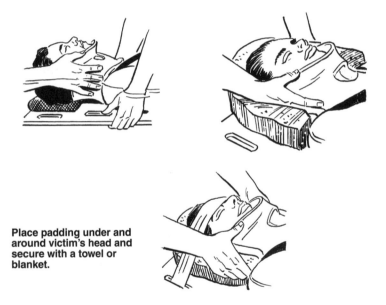

Place padding under and around victim's head and secure with a towel or blanket.

Removal from Water

- Once the victim is secured on the board, remove him from the water. The rescuer at his head should direct the removal.

- If in a pool, move the victim to the side of the pool. Position the board perpendicular to the side of the pool. The board should be kept as horizontal as possible while it is being removed.

- Remove the board head-first. You might have to tip the board at the head to break the initial suction holding it in the water.

- If emergency help has arrived they will be able to help in the removal of the victim.

- Two people should be on the deck to help lift and slide the board onto the deck. The person at the victim's head can either move to the deck or help at the sides, depending on available help. The board and victim are removed slowly and carefully.

- Once the victim is removed from the water, give first aid for shock.

- Continue to monitor the victim's consciousness and breathing.

Removal from water

Resuscitation of Drowning Victims

Resuscitation is a general term that covers all of the measures taken to restore life or consciousness to an individual who is apparently dead. These measures include rescue breathing to restore normal breathing, and external heart compression to maintain blood circulation. Mouth-to-mouth or mouth-to-nose resuscitation should be started at once in any case of stopped breathing. This is often the only step needed for the victim of a drowning.

Only after resuscitation has been started and after it has been determined that the heart has stopped, should external heart compression be started. External cardiac compression must always be accompanied by mouth-to-mouth resuscitation. The complete procedure is called cardiopulmonary resuscitation (CPR).

Complete CPR should be attempted only by persons qualified by practice under the supervision of a certified instructor. Practice only on a mannequin; severe injury can result if CPR is performed on a person whose heart is functioning. If you have the opportunity to take a course in CPR before starting Lifesaving merit badge, don't delay. You will be that much ahead and you might save a life in the intervening period. At the beginning of this pamphlet we noted that some skills will require practice throughout your life. CPR is one of these. If it has been over a year since you received your training, a refresher course might be needed. These are offered by numerous organizations in your community. Also explore the possibility of more advanced training. Some important techniques are not covered in the basic courses currently required for the merit badge.

Conclusion

We have discussed a number of subjects, from line rescues to underwater searches, to tired-swimmer assists, all under the heading of *go* rescues. It is necessary for you to know all of these skills to be prepared for the widest assortment of circumstances. Never forget, however, that the swimming rescue is the last in the *order of methods,* preceded by *reach, throw,* and *row.* The lifesaver who disregards a simpler technique in favor of a swimming rescue is like a race car driver who refuses to wear a seat belt and crash helmet. No one doubts his skills, but his judgment is poor. Develop all of your skills and rely on them in time of need, but do not take unnecessary chances, if not for your own sake, then for the sake of the person you are trying to save.

Every year people drown trying to save someone else. In many cases, they are frantic friends and relatives whose swimming skills and rescue training are no better than those of the person in distress. They swim to the victim because they know of no other way. You do; don't repeat their mistake. Chances are, of course, that you could handle the victim in the water. After all, we have discussed techniques for doing just that. However, double drownings prove that a struggling victim is not to be taken lightly. Your training should be used for one purpose only, saving lives; not to impress anyone with your prowess. There is nothing cowardly or unheroic about using a simple rescue whenever possible. There is definitely something foolhardy or ill-informed about doing it any other way.

The Lifesaving merit badge should prepare you for most emergencies encountered by the casual swimmer. However, no matter how extensive your previous training, you can always be better prepared. Take the opportunity to attend courses offered by other organizations and investigate the other aquatic merit badges to further your boating rescue skills. Keep your skills fresh by continued practice. You might also wish to become a candidate for BSA Lifeguard. This special Scout certification will give you practice in lifeguarding, boat rescues, and advanced rescue skills. It is an excellent way to qualify for summer camp staff. Check with your Scoutmaster or local council service center for names of approved BSA Lifeguard counselors.